Omelets, Waffles, and More: 50 Brunch Classics

By: Kelly Johnson

Table of Contents

- Avocado Toast with Poached Egg
- Banana Oat Pancakes
- Greek Yogurt Parfait with Granola
- Spinach and Mushroom Scramble
- Overnight Chia Pudding
- Sweet Potato Hash with Eggs
- Blueberry Almond Smoothie
- Classic French Toast
- Breakfast Burrito with Salsa
- Cottage Cheese and Fresh Fruit Bowl
- Protein-Packed Smoothie Bowl
- Scrambled Eggs with Smoked Salmon
- Coconut Banana Bread
- Whole Wheat Waffles with Berries
- Veggie Breakfast Quesadilla
- Classic Breakfast Burrito
- Zucchini Frittata
- Apple Cinnamon Oatmeal
- Smoked Salmon Bagel with Cream Cheese
- Tofu Scramble with Veggies
- Peanut Butter and Banana Smoothie
- Sweet Cornmeal Pancakes
- Chocolate Chip Banana Muffins
- Avocado and Tomato Breakfast Salad
- Smashed Chickpea Toast
- Chia Seed Granola Bars
- Ham and Cheese Croissant Sandwich
- Almond Butter and Banana Smoothie
- Porridge with Maple Syrup and Walnuts
- Breakfast Tacos with Scrambled Eggs
- Quinoa Breakfast Bowl
- Egg and Spinach Breakfast Wrap
- Mango Coconut Smoothie
- Poached Eggs with Sautéed Kale
- Blueberry Chia Jam on Toast

- Oatmeal with Berries and Almonds
- Egg Muffins with Vegetables
- Avocado Smoothie
- Bacon and Egg Breakfast Cups
- Cinnamon Apple Quinoa Bowl
- Breakfast Sandwich with Avocado
- Pumpkin Spice Smoothie
- Cucumber and Cream Cheese Sandwich
- Breakfast Polenta with Tomato and Egg
- Grilled Peach and Ricotta Toast
- Tofu and Avocado Breakfast Wrap
- Sourdough Toast with Almond Butter
- Protein Pancakes with Berries
- Carrot Cake Oatmeal
- Roasted Tomato and Basil Frittata

Avocado Toast with Poached Egg

Ingredients:

- 1 slice of whole-grain bread, toasted
- 1/2 ripe avocado
- 1 large egg
- 1 teaspoon vinegar
- Salt and pepper to taste
- Red chili flakes or everything bagel seasoning (optional)

Instructions:

1. Mash the avocado onto the toasted bread. Season with salt and pepper.
2. In a small pot, bring water to a gentle simmer and add vinegar.
3. Crack the egg into a small bowl, then carefully slide it into the simmering water. Cook for 3-4 minutes for a runny yolk.
4. Remove the poached egg with a slotted spoon and place it on top of the avocado toast.
5. Sprinkle with chili flakes or seasoning, if desired. Serve immediately.

Banana Oat Pancakes

Ingredients:

- 1 ripe banana
- 1/2 cup rolled oats
- 2 large eggs
- 1/4 teaspoon cinnamon
- 1/4 teaspoon baking powder
- Cooking spray or butter for frying

Instructions:

1. Blend the banana, oats, eggs, cinnamon, and baking powder in a blender until smooth.
2. Heat a non-stick skillet over medium heat and lightly grease with cooking spray or butter.
3. Pour small amounts of batter onto the skillet to form pancakes. Cook for 2-3 minutes per side until golden brown.
4. Serve with your favorite toppings like maple syrup, berries, or yogurt.

Greek Yogurt Parfait with Granola

Ingredients:

- 1 cup Greek yogurt
- 1/2 cup granola
- 1/2 cup mixed berries (strawberries, blueberries, raspberries)
- 1 tablespoon honey or maple syrup (optional)

Instructions:

1. Layer half of the Greek yogurt in a glass or bowl.
2. Add a layer of granola and mixed berries.
3. Repeat the layers with the remaining yogurt, granola, and berries.
4. Drizzle with honey or maple syrup, if desired. Serve immediately.

Spinach and Mushroom Scramble

Ingredients:

- 2 large eggs
- 1/4 cup milk or water
- 1/2 cup spinach, chopped
- 1/4 cup mushrooms, sliced
- 1 tablespoon olive oil or butter
- Salt and pepper to taste

Instructions:

1. In a bowl, whisk the eggs with milk or water and season with salt and pepper.
2. Heat olive oil or butter in a skillet over medium heat. Add mushrooms and sauté for 2-3 minutes.
3. Add spinach and cook until wilted, about 1 minute.
4. Pour the egg mixture into the skillet and gently stir until eggs are cooked to your desired consistency. Serve immediately.

Overnight Chia Pudding

Ingredients:

- 1/4 cup chia seeds
- 1 cup milk (or milk substitute)
- 1 tablespoon maple syrup or honey
- 1/2 teaspoon vanilla extract
- Fresh fruits or nuts for topping

Instructions:

1. In a jar or bowl, mix chia seeds, milk, maple syrup, and vanilla extract. Stir well.
2. Cover and refrigerate overnight or for at least 4 hours.
3. Stir again before serving and top with fresh fruits or nuts. Serve cold.

Sweet Potato Hash with Eggs

Ingredients:

- 1 medium sweet potato, diced
- 1/4 cup onion, diced
- 1/4 cup bell pepper, diced
- 2 large eggs
- 1 tablespoon olive oil
- Salt, pepper, and paprika to taste

Instructions:

1. Heat olive oil in a skillet over medium heat. Add sweet potatoes and cook for 5-7 minutes until slightly softened.
2. Add onions and bell peppers and cook until tender, about 5 minutes. Season with salt, pepper, and paprika.
3. Make two small wells in the hash and crack an egg into each. Cover and cook until eggs reach desired doneness. Serve immediately.

Blueberry Almond Smoothie

Ingredients:

- 1 cup frozen blueberries
- 1/2 banana
- 1/2 cup almond milk
- 1 tablespoon almond butter
- 1/2 teaspoon vanilla extract
- Ice cubes (optional)

Instructions:

1. Combine all ingredients in a blender and blend until smooth.
2. Add ice cubes if you prefer a thicker smoothie. Serve immediately.

Classic French Toast

Ingredients:

- 2 slices of bread
- 1 large egg
- 1/4 cup milk
- 1/4 teaspoon cinnamon
- 1/2 teaspoon vanilla extract
- Butter for cooking
- Maple syrup or powdered sugar for serving

Instructions:

1. In a shallow dish, whisk together the egg, milk, cinnamon, and vanilla.
2. Dip each slice of bread into the mixture, coating both sides.
3. Heat a skillet over medium heat and add butter. Cook the bread slices for 2-3 minutes per side until golden brown.
4. Serve with maple syrup or powdered sugar. Enjoy!

Breakfast Burrito with Salsa

Ingredients:

- 2 large tortillas
- 2 large eggs
- 1/4 cup black beans, rinsed
- 1/4 cup shredded cheese
- 1/4 cup diced tomatoes
- 1/4 cup salsa
- 1/4 avocado, sliced
- 1 tablespoon olive oil
- Salt and pepper to taste

Instructions:

1. Heat olive oil in a skillet over medium heat. Scramble the eggs and season with salt and pepper.
2. Warm the tortillas in a separate pan or microwave.
3. Fill each tortilla with scrambled eggs, black beans, cheese, tomatoes, and avocado.
4. Roll the tortillas into burritos and serve with salsa on the side.

Cottage Cheese and Fresh Fruit Bowl

Ingredients:

- 1 cup cottage cheese
- 1/2 cup fresh fruit (berries, diced melon, or pineapple)
- 1 tablespoon honey (optional)
- 1 tablespoon granola or nuts (optional)

Instructions:

1. Spoon cottage cheese into a bowl.
2. Top with fresh fruit and drizzle with honey, if desired.
3. Sprinkle granola or nuts on top for extra crunch. Serve chilled.

Protein-Packed Smoothie Bowl

Ingredients:

- 1 frozen banana
- 1/2 cup Greek yogurt
- 1/2 cup almond milk
- 1 scoop protein powder (optional)
- 1 tablespoon peanut butter
- Toppings: granola, sliced fruit, chia seeds

Instructions:

1. Blend banana, yogurt, almond milk, protein powder, and peanut butter until smooth.
2. Pour the mixture into a bowl and top with your choice of granola, sliced fruit, and chia seeds. Serve immediately.

Scrambled Eggs with Smoked Salmon

Ingredients:

- 2 large eggs
- 2 tablespoons milk
- 1/4 cup smoked salmon, chopped
- 1 tablespoon butter
- Salt and pepper to taste
- Chopped chives for garnish

Instructions:

1. Whisk eggs with milk, salt, and pepper.
2. Melt butter in a skillet over medium heat. Add the egg mixture and gently stir until scrambled.
3. Stir in smoked salmon and cook for an additional 1-2 minutes. Garnish with chives and serve.

Coconut Banana Bread

Ingredients:

- 2 ripe bananas, mashed
- 1/2 cup coconut oil, melted
- 2 large eggs
- 1/2 cup sugar
- 1 3/4 cups all-purpose flour
- 1 teaspoon baking soda
- 1/4 teaspoon salt
- 1/2 cup shredded coconut

Instructions:

1. Preheat oven to 350°F (175°C) and grease a loaf pan.
2. Mix mashed bananas, coconut oil, eggs, and sugar in a bowl.
3. In another bowl, combine flour, baking soda, and salt. Gradually add to the wet ingredients. Fold in shredded coconut.
4. Pour the batter into the loaf pan and bake for 50-60 minutes, or until a toothpick inserted into the center comes out clean. Cool before slicing.

Whole Wheat Waffles with Berries

Ingredients:

- 1 cup whole wheat flour
- 1 teaspoon baking powder
- 1/2 teaspoon cinnamon
- 1 large egg
- 1 cup milk
- 2 tablespoons melted butter
- Fresh berries and syrup for topping

Instructions:

1. Preheat your waffle iron.
2. In a bowl, whisk together flour, baking powder, and cinnamon.
3. In another bowl, mix the egg, milk, and melted butter. Add wet ingredients to the dry ingredients and mix until smooth.
4. Cook waffles according to your waffle iron's instructions. Serve topped with fresh berries and syrup.

Veggie Breakfast Quesadilla

Ingredients:

- 1 large tortilla
- 1/4 cup shredded cheese
- 1/4 cup diced bell peppers
- 1/4 cup spinach, chopped
- 1 egg, scrambled
- 1 tablespoon olive oil

Instructions:

1. Heat olive oil in a skillet and sauté bell peppers and spinach until softened.
2. Lay the tortilla flat and sprinkle half the cheese on one side. Add the veggies, scrambled egg, and remaining cheese. Fold the tortilla in half.
3. Cook in the skillet over medium heat until the tortilla is golden and the cheese is melted. Slice and serve.

Classic Breakfast Burrito

Ingredients:

- 2 large tortillas
- 2 scrambled eggs
- 1/4 cup cooked sausage or bacon
- 1/4 cup shredded cheese
- 1/4 cup diced potatoes or hash browns
- Salsa for serving

Instructions:

1. Fill each tortilla with scrambled eggs, sausage or bacon, cheese, and potatoes.
2. Roll the tortillas tightly into burritos.
3. Heat the burritos in a skillet for 1-2 minutes per side until warmed. Serve with salsa.

Zucchini Frittata

Ingredients:

- 1 medium zucchini, grated
- 4 large eggs
- 1/4 cup milk
- 1/4 cup shredded cheese
- 1 tablespoon olive oil
- Salt and pepper to taste

Instructions:

1. Preheat the oven to 375°F (190°C).
2. In a bowl, whisk eggs, milk, salt, and pepper. Stir in zucchini and cheese.
3. Heat olive oil in an oven-safe skillet over medium heat. Pour in the egg mixture and cook for 2-3 minutes.
4. Transfer the skillet to the oven and bake for 15 minutes, or until set. Slice and serve.

Apple Cinnamon Oatmeal

Ingredients:

- 1 cup rolled oats
- 2 cups water or milk
- 1 apple, diced
- 1/2 teaspoon cinnamon
- 1 tablespoon honey (optional)
- 1/4 cup chopped nuts (optional)
- 1/4 cup raisins or dried cranberries (optional)

Instructions:

1. In a medium saucepan, bring water or milk to a boil. Add oats and reduce to a simmer. Cook for 5-7 minutes, stirring occasionally.
2. Add diced apple, cinnamon, and honey to the oats and cook for an additional 2-3 minutes, until apples are tender.
3. Top with nuts and dried fruit, if desired, and serve warm.

Smoked Salmon Bagel with Cream Cheese

Ingredients:

- 1 bagel, halved
- 2 tablespoons cream cheese
- 4-5 slices smoked salmon
- 1/4 red onion, thinly sliced
- Capers (optional)
- Fresh dill for garnish

Instructions:

1. Toast the bagel halves to your preference.
2. Spread cream cheese on each half.
3. Layer smoked salmon on top, followed by red onion slices and capers, if using.
4. Garnish with fresh dill and serve immediately.

Tofu Scramble with Veggies

Ingredients:

- 1 block firm tofu, drained and crumbled
- 1/4 cup bell pepper, diced
- 1/4 cup onion, diced
- 1/4 cup spinach, chopped
- 1 tablespoon olive oil
- 1/2 teaspoon turmeric
- Salt and pepper to taste

Instructions:

1. Heat olive oil in a skillet over medium heat. Add bell pepper and onion, and sauté until softened.
2. Add crumbled tofu, turmeric, salt, and pepper. Stir well and cook for 5-7 minutes, allowing the tofu to absorb the flavors.
3. Stir in spinach and cook for another 2 minutes, until wilted. Serve hot.

Peanut Butter and Banana Smoothie

Ingredients:

- 1 ripe banana
- 1 tablespoon peanut butter
- 1/2 cup almond milk (or any milk of choice)
- 1/2 cup Greek yogurt
- 1 tablespoon honey (optional)

Instructions:

1. Add banana, peanut butter, almond milk, Greek yogurt, and honey to a blender.
2. Blend until smooth.
3. Pour into a glass and serve immediately.

Sweet Cornmeal Pancakes

Ingredients:

- 1 cup cornmeal
- 1/2 cup all-purpose flour
- 1 tablespoon sugar
- 1 teaspoon baking powder
- 1/2 teaspoon salt
- 1 cup milk
- 2 large eggs
- 2 tablespoons melted butter

Instructions:

1. In a bowl, whisk together cornmeal, flour, sugar, baking powder, and salt.
2. In a separate bowl, whisk milk, eggs, and melted butter.
3. Combine the wet and dry ingredients and stir until smooth.
4. Heat a skillet or griddle over medium heat and lightly grease with butter or oil.
5. Pour the batter onto the skillet and cook pancakes until bubbles form on the surface. Flip and cook for another 2 minutes. Serve with syrup or fresh fruit.

Chocolate Chip Banana Muffins

Ingredients:

- 2 ripe bananas, mashed
- 1/2 cup sugar
- 1/4 cup melted butter
- 1 egg
- 1 teaspoon vanilla extract
- 1 1/2 cups all-purpose flour
- 1 teaspoon baking soda
- 1/2 teaspoon salt
- 1/2 cup chocolate chips

Instructions:

1. Preheat the oven to 350°F (175°C). Line a muffin tin with paper liners.
2. In a large bowl, combine mashed bananas, sugar, melted butter, egg, and vanilla extract.
3. In a separate bowl, whisk together flour, baking soda, and salt. Gradually add the dry ingredients to the wet ingredients and stir until combined.
4. Fold in chocolate chips.
5. Divide the batter evenly among the muffin cups and bake for 18-20 minutes, or until a toothpick comes out clean. Let cool before serving.

Avocado and Tomato Breakfast Salad

Ingredients:

- 1 ripe avocado, diced
- 1/2 cup cherry tomatoes, halved
- 1/4 red onion, thinly sliced
- 1 tablespoon olive oil
- 1 tablespoon balsamic vinegar
- Salt and pepper to taste

Instructions:

1. In a bowl, combine diced avocado, cherry tomatoes, and red onion.
2. Drizzle with olive oil and balsamic vinegar. Toss gently to combine.
3. Season with salt and pepper and serve immediately.

Smashed Chickpea Toast

Ingredients:

- 1/2 cup canned chickpeas, rinsed and drained
- 1 tablespoon olive oil
- 1 tablespoon lemon juice
- 1/4 teaspoon garlic powder
- Salt and pepper to taste
- 2 slices whole-grain bread, toasted
- Fresh parsley for garnish

Instructions:

1. Mash chickpeas in a bowl using a fork or potato masher.
2. Stir in olive oil, lemon juice, garlic powder, salt, and pepper.
3. Spread the smashed chickpea mixture on toasted bread.
4. Garnish with fresh parsley and serve immediately.

Chia Seed Granola Bars

Ingredients:

- 1 1/2 cups rolled oats
- 1/4 cup chia seeds
- 1/2 cup mixed nuts, chopped
- 1/4 cup honey or maple syrup
- 1/4 cup almond butter
- 1/2 teaspoon vanilla extract
- 1/4 cup dried fruit (optional)

Instructions:

1. Preheat the oven to 325°F (165°C). Line a baking dish with parchment paper.
2. In a large bowl, mix oats, chia seeds, nuts, and dried fruit.
3. In a small saucepan, warm honey or maple syrup and almond butter over low heat until combined. Add vanilla extract.
4. Pour the wet mixture into the dry ingredients and mix until fully coated.
5. Press the mixture firmly into the baking dish and bake for 20-25 minutes. Let cool completely before cutting into bars.

Ham and Cheese Croissant Sandwich

Ingredients:

- 2 croissants, halved
- 4 slices deli ham
- 4 slices Swiss or cheddar cheese
- 1 tablespoon Dijon mustard (optional)

Instructions:

1. Preheat your oven to 375°F (190°C).
2. Spread mustard on the bottom half of each croissant (optional).
3. Layer ham and cheese on each croissant half, then place the top half on.
4. Wrap the sandwiches in foil and bake for 10-12 minutes, or until the cheese is melted. Serve warm.

Almond Butter and Banana Smoothie

Ingredients:

- 1 ripe banana
- 2 tablespoons almond butter
- 1 cup almond milk
- 1/2 teaspoon cinnamon
- 1 tablespoon honey (optional)
- Ice cubes

Instructions:

1. Add all ingredients to a blender.
2. Blend until smooth.
3. Pour into a glass and enjoy immediately.

Porridge with Maple Syrup and Walnuts

Ingredients:

- 1 cup rolled oats
- 2 cups milk or water
- 1/4 cup chopped walnuts
- 2 tablespoons maple syrup
- 1/2 teaspoon cinnamon

Instructions:

1. In a saucepan, bring milk or water to a boil. Add oats and reduce to a simmer. Cook for 5-7 minutes, stirring occasionally.
2. Serve in a bowl, topped with walnuts, maple syrup, and a sprinkle of cinnamon.

Breakfast Tacos with Scrambled Eggs

Ingredients:

- 4 small flour or corn tortillas
- 4 eggs, beaten
- 1/4 cup shredded cheese
- 1/4 cup diced tomatoes
- 1/4 cup chopped cilantro
- Salsa (optional)
- Salt and pepper to taste

Instructions:

1. Heat a skillet over medium heat and scramble the eggs until cooked. Season with salt and pepper.
2. Warm tortillas in a pan or microwave.
3. Divide the eggs among the tortillas and top with cheese, tomatoes, and cilantro. Add salsa if desired. Serve immediately.

Quinoa Breakfast Bowl

Ingredients:

- 1 cup cooked quinoa
- 1/2 cup almond milk
- 1 tablespoon honey or maple syrup
- 1/4 cup fresh berries
- 1 tablespoon chopped nuts
- 1/2 teaspoon cinnamon

Instructions:

1. Warm the cooked quinoa in a small saucepan with almond milk. Stir in honey or maple syrup and cinnamon.
2. Transfer to a bowl and top with fresh berries and nuts. Serve warm.

Egg and Spinach Breakfast Wrap

Ingredients:

- 2 large eggs, beaten
- 1/2 cup fresh spinach
- 1 whole-grain tortilla
- 1/4 cup shredded cheese
- Salt and pepper to taste

Instructions:

1. Heat a skillet over medium heat and cook the eggs, stirring gently, until scrambled. Add spinach and cook until wilted.
2. Place the scrambled eggs and spinach onto the tortilla. Sprinkle with cheese and roll up tightly. Serve immediately.

Mango Coconut Smoothie

Ingredients:

- 1 cup fresh or frozen mango chunks
- 1/2 cup coconut milk
- 1/2 cup Greek yogurt
- 1 tablespoon honey (optional)
- Ice cubes

Instructions:

1. Add mango, coconut milk, Greek yogurt, honey, and ice cubes to a blender.
2. Blend until smooth.
3. Pour into a glass and enjoy.

Poached Eggs with Sautéed Kale

Ingredients:

- 2 large eggs
- 2 cups fresh kale, chopped
- 1 tablespoon olive oil
- 1 clove garlic, minced
- Salt and pepper to taste
- Red pepper flakes (optional)

Instructions:

1. Heat olive oil in a skillet over medium heat. Add garlic and sauté until fragrant. Add kale and cook until wilted. Season with salt, pepper, and red pepper flakes if desired.
2. Bring a pot of water to a gentle simmer. Crack an egg into a small bowl and gently slide it into the water. Repeat with the second egg. Poach for 3-4 minutes.
3. Serve the poached eggs over the sautéed kale. Enjoy warm.

Blueberry Chia Jam on Toast

Ingredients:

- 1 cup fresh or frozen blueberries
- 2 tablespoons chia seeds
- 1 tablespoon honey or maple syrup
- Whole-grain bread, toasted

Instructions:

1. In a saucepan, heat blueberries over medium heat until they start to break down. Mash with a fork.
2. Stir in chia seeds and honey. Simmer for 5 minutes, stirring occasionally. Let cool to thicken.
3. Spread the chia jam on toasted bread and serve.

Oatmeal with Berries and Almonds

Ingredients:

- 1/2 cup rolled oats
- 1 cup milk or water
- 1/4 cup fresh berries (e.g., blueberries, raspberries)
- 1 tablespoon sliced almonds
- 1 teaspoon honey or maple syrup

Instructions:

1. Cook oats in milk or water according to package instructions.
2. Transfer to a bowl and top with berries, almonds, and honey. Serve warm.

Egg Muffins with Vegetables

Ingredients:

- 6 large eggs
- 1/2 cup diced bell peppers
- 1/2 cup spinach, chopped
- 1/4 cup shredded cheese
- Salt and pepper to taste

Instructions:

1. Preheat the oven to 375°F (190°C). Grease a muffin tin.
2. In a bowl, whisk eggs and season with salt and pepper. Add vegetables and cheese.
3. Pour the mixture into the muffin tin, filling each cup about 3/4 full.
4. Bake for 18-20 minutes, or until set. Cool slightly before serving.

Avocado Smoothie

Ingredients:

- 1 ripe avocado, peeled and pitted
- 1 cup almond milk
- 1 tablespoon honey
- 1/2 teaspoon vanilla extract
- Ice cubes

Instructions:

1. Combine all ingredients in a blender.
2. Blend until smooth.
3. Pour into a glass and serve immediately.

Bacon and Egg Breakfast Cups

Ingredients:

- 6 slices of bacon
- 6 large eggs
- Salt and pepper to taste
- Fresh parsley for garnish (optional)

Instructions:

1. Preheat the oven to 375°F (190°C). Grease a muffin tin.
2. Line each muffin cup with a slice of bacon.
3. Crack an egg into each bacon-lined cup. Season with salt and pepper.
4. Bake for 12-15 minutes, or until the eggs are cooked to your liking. Garnish with parsley if desired.

Cinnamon Apple Quinoa Bowl

Ingredients:

- 1 cup cooked quinoa
- 1/2 cup diced apple
- 1/4 teaspoon cinnamon
- 1 tablespoon honey
- 1/4 cup almond milk

Instructions:

1. In a saucepan, warm quinoa, apple, cinnamon, and almond milk over low heat.
2. Stir in honey and cook until heated through.
3. Serve in a bowl and enjoy warm.

Breakfast Sandwich with Avocado

Ingredients:

- 2 slices whole-grain bread, toasted
- 1/2 avocado, mashed
- 1 fried egg
- 1 slice tomato
- Salt and pepper to taste

Instructions:

1. Spread mashed avocado on one slice of toast.
2. Layer with tomato and the fried egg. Season with salt and pepper.
3. Top with the second slice of toast. Serve immediately.

Pumpkin Spice Smoothie

Ingredients:

- 1/2 cup pumpkin puree
- 1 banana
- 1 cup almond milk
- 1/2 teaspoon pumpkin pie spice
- 1 tablespoon honey (optional)
- Ice cubes

Instructions:

1. Add all ingredients to a blender.
2. Blend until smooth.
3. Pour into a glass and garnish with a sprinkle of pumpkin pie spice if desired.

Cucumber and Cream Cheese Sandwich

Ingredients:

- 2 slices whole-grain bread
- 2 tablespoons cream cheese
- 1/4 cucumber, thinly sliced
- Salt and pepper to taste

Instructions:

1. Spread cream cheese evenly on both slices of bread.
2. Layer cucumber slices on one slice of bread.
3. Sprinkle with salt and pepper. Top with the second slice of bread.
4. Cut into halves or quarters and serve.

Breakfast Polenta with Tomato and Egg

Ingredients:

- 1/2 cup polenta
- 2 cups water or milk
- 1 tablespoon butter
- 1/2 cup cherry tomatoes, halved
- 1 fried or poached egg
- Salt and pepper to taste
- Fresh basil for garnish

Instructions:

1. Cook polenta according to package instructions, stirring frequently. Add butter and season with salt.
2. Sauté cherry tomatoes in a skillet until softened.
3. Spoon polenta into a bowl, top with tomatoes and egg. Garnish with fresh basil and serve warm.

Grilled Peach and Ricotta Toast

Ingredients:

- 2 slices of sourdough bread
- 1 ripe peach, halved and pitted
- 2 tablespoons ricotta cheese
- Honey for drizzling
- Fresh mint leaves for garnish

Instructions:

1. Grill peach halves until slightly charred and softened. Slice into wedges.
2. Toast sourdough bread and spread with ricotta.
3. Top with grilled peaches, drizzle with honey, and garnish with mint leaves. Serve immediately.

Tofu and Avocado Breakfast Wrap

Ingredients:

- 1 large tortilla
- 1/2 block firm tofu, crumbled
- 1/4 avocado, sliced
- 1/4 cup spinach leaves
- 1 tablespoon olive oil
- 1/2 teaspoon turmeric
- Salt and pepper to taste

Instructions:

1. Heat olive oil in a skillet. Add tofu and turmeric, cooking until warmed through. Season with salt and pepper.
2. Lay spinach, tofu, and avocado on the tortilla.
3. Roll tightly into a wrap. Serve immediately or warm slightly in the skillet.

Sourdough Toast with Almond Butter

Ingredients:

- 2 slices sourdough bread, toasted
- 2 tablespoons almond butter
- 1 teaspoon honey
- A sprinkle of chia seeds

Instructions:

1. Spread almond butter evenly on toasted sourdough.
2. Drizzle with honey and sprinkle with chia seeds. Serve immediately.

Protein Pancakes with Berries

Ingredients:

- 1/2 cup rolled oats
- 1/2 cup cottage cheese
- 2 large eggs
- 1/2 teaspoon baking powder
- 1/2 teaspoon vanilla extract
- Fresh berries for topping

Instructions:

1. Blend oats, cottage cheese, eggs, baking powder, and vanilla until smooth.
2. Heat a non-stick skillet over medium heat. Pour batter to form small pancakes.
3. Cook for 2-3 minutes on each side. Top with fresh berries and serve.

Carrot Cake Oatmeal

Ingredients:

- 1/2 cup rolled oats
- 1 cup almond milk or water
- 1/4 cup grated carrot
- 1/2 teaspoon cinnamon
- 1 tablespoon maple syrup
- 1 tablespoon chopped walnuts

Instructions:

1. Cook oats with almond milk and grated carrot over medium heat. Stir frequently.
2. Add cinnamon and maple syrup. Cook until creamy.
3. Serve topped with walnuts and a drizzle of maple syrup.

Roasted Tomato and Basil Frittata

Ingredients:

- 6 large eggs
- 1/2 cup cherry tomatoes, halved
- 1/4 cup fresh basil, chopped
- 1/4 cup grated Parmesan cheese
- 1 tablespoon olive oil
- Salt and pepper to taste

Instructions:

1. Preheat oven to 375°F (190°C). Heat olive oil in an oven-safe skillet.
2. Sauté tomatoes until slightly softened.
3. Beat eggs with Parmesan, basil, salt, and pepper. Pour over tomatoes.

4. Cook on the stovetop until edges set, then transfer to the oven. Bake for 10-12 minutes or until fully set. Serve warm.

www.ingramcontent.com/pod-product-compliance
Lightning Source LLC
LaVergne TN
LVHW081508060526
838201LV00056BA/3002